Morning
MEDITATIONS

SIDNEY S. WILLIAMS, JR.

FIRST EDITION

ISBN: 978-1-939748-60-7

Published by

P.O. Box 2839, Apopka, FL 32704

Printed in the United States of America

Disclaimer: The views and opinions expressed in this book are solely those of the authors and other contributors. These views and opinions do not necessarily represent those of Certa Publishing.

Table of Contents

Dedication

*Dedicated to the memory of my mother, Mina,
whose early morning phone calls I dearly miss.*

This book would not have been possible without the support and encouragement of my wife, Teresa and our children, Nicole, Sarah, Hannah, and Sidney III. I am especially thankful for the many people who took time to let me know how much my morning meditations inspired them and who inspired me to write this book. Words cannot express how grateful I am to Victoria Howze for compiling more than three years of my morning mediations.

Foreword

by Rev. Dr. Jessica K. Ingram

*I*n the June 1982 in the city of Chicago, I clearly heard God speaking to me and giving me instructions on how I should begin my day. I struggled with depression because I felt like such a failure. It seemed that no matter what I tried, nothing really worked. Through the years I have learned that God has a way of interrupting our daily routine and habits and attempting to speak to us. For us, the challenge is to be attentive to God's voice, to recognize when God speaks and to follow the instructions that are given. This is what I needed on that life changing morning.

On that morning, I heard God's voice. God said to me, "You are so busy working for me, but you don't know me because you do not spend time with me." I was blown away! I was faithfully working for God and yet the God for whom I was working told me that I did not really know Him. As God continued to speak He said to me, "You don't know me because you do not spend set aside time with me. I want you to start having morning meditations every day. I want you to spend quality time with me." I knew this was God speaking to me because I knew my soul was dying. I heeded the instructions and started spending time with Him in my early morning meditations.

For the past thirty plus years I have been in the habit of getting up early and spending time with God. It has been my practice to get centered, listen to worship music, write in my journal, read meditation books, the bible and praying. Establishing this spiritual discipline has had a profound effect on my life. Because of this discipline I have been able to overcome numerous challenges. I know without a doubt, my time with God in the morning has made the difference.

The meditation books that I read have enhanced my morning journey. Authors like Dallas Willard, Brennan Manning, Henri Nouwen, and Joan Chittitister have provided me with much spiritual insight, each one seeming to say exactly what I needed to hear for that day. I am blessed to be able to add to my list of favorite books and writers, Rev. Sidney S. Williams Jr. Rev. Williams has produced a necessary work for anyone who wants to enhance their meditation life. I like the title of the book, "Morning Meditations." It lets me know the importance of starting your day with God. Each day there is a brief thought and yet these few sentences give profound insight that is needed for each day. Everyone needs something to "jump start their day." Morning Meditations does just that. Time spent reading Rev. Williams work will change your perspective and give you exactly what you need to face each day and know that God is truly with you.

I commend the Rev. Sidney Williams Jr. for taking the time to write a meditation book. As a pastor, a husband and a father of four, his plate is full; yet he is not too busy to start his day with God. Rev. Sidney understands what a difference this time with God has made in his life. He would love to share this with you.

Read and watch your day change.

Rev. Dr. Jessica Kendall Ingram

Preface

Throughout my childhood, I was taught that I had to be better and smarter than my peers to be successful. Consequently, when I became an adult my definition of success was always relative to others - comparing myself to those who ascended the corporate ladder the fastest or who amassed the most wealth. The pressure to succeed (or the fear of failure) caused me to take unnecessary risks for the hope of an even greater reward, such as power, wealth and status. Ironically, the thrill on the road to success is often riddled with fear and the feeling of having no safety net. [A safety net is designed to catch someone who falls, such as an acrobat from a circus trapeze; or, metaphorically, to provide a sense of physical, professional, or financial security.] What happens if there really isn't a safety net? How, then, should success be viewed?

My achievements were invisible to me because of my fear of failure. I lost the ability to look at my past as a success story in and of itself. Whenever I started something new, I would be overwhelmed with thoughts of failing, and I would begin to sabotage myself by believing the people in my present situation will behave as those in my past. This presented real challenges for me in my career and my marriage, but no one could help me figure out who was at the root of my problem, because the problem had been created in my mind. In my journey toward believing I am successful, I have discovered four essential elements to getting rid of my fears:

1. Looking back over my life is critical to seeing how God is with me every step along the way.
2. Developing relationships with the people I meet rather than competing with them.
3. Seeking opportunities to build with people rather than using people as a means to an uncertain end.
4. Framing success with a transformed mind and a new paradigm.

This book is written to help you in the first 100 days of your new assignment or your first 100 days to a new outlook on life. As you prepare for bed each night, meditate on how the day moved you one step closer to true success. When you awake each day, take to time read and reflect on the Morning Meditation to frame your new day.

Joshua 1:8 "This book of the law shall not depart out of thy mouth; but thou shalt meditate therein day and night, that thou mayest observe to do according to all that is written therein: for then thou shalt make thy way prosperous, and then thou shalt have good success."

Defining the Goal

Day 1

Morning Meditation:

*P*eople often associate success with luck or divine intervention, but the reality is that successful people invest more than 12,000 unpaid hours in a particular area to become the best at what they do. Confucius taught that when the student is ready, the teacher will appear. Jesus called it the cost of discipleship. How much will you sacrifice to become the best at what you are called to do?

Read Luke 14:25-33.

_____

_____

_____

_____

_____

_____

_____

Day 2

Morning Meditation:

*F*ew people will ever reach their potential because of their anxiety about their present circumstances and their fear of their past. To unlock your potential, you will have to embrace the supernatural and rise above your circumstances. Your future can only be activated by your faith; without faith you will remain in the bondage of your past.

Read Mathew 6:33-34

Day 3

Morning Meditation:

*T*he words "I am" should always introduce our future state of being if we are Christians and not our present condition. Let's give it a try today! "I am _____ ."

Read Exodus 3:14-15

_____

_____

_____

_____

_____

_____

_____

_____

_____

_____

_____

Day 4

Morning Meditation:

If you want to be successful in this life, then find something greater than yourself to become knowledgeable about.

Read 2 Timothy 2:15

_____
_____
_____
_____
_____
_____
_____
_____
_____
_____
_____
_____

Day 5

Morning Meditation:

*T*he secret of success is learning to stop chasing the next level or the next promotion. We must learn to be content with mastering the level we are currently on and trust God for the increase. Remember, life is lived in the valley not on the mountaintop.

Read Joshua 1:8, Matthew 23:12

_____

_____

_____

_____

_____

_____

_____

_____

_____

Day 6

Morning Meditation:

$\mathcal{G}$reatness cannot be grasped in the human mind because of our obsession with our own imperfections and our dependence on the approval of others, but there is greatness in all of us that is not dependent on what we do. We are great in God's mind and our challenge is to see ourselves from God's point of view.

Read 1 Corinthians 2:9

_____

_____

_____

_____

_____

_____

_____

_____

Day 7

Morning Meditation:

*S*uccess breeds contempt among your peers because it appears that you made it overnight while your peers have been diligently working toward the same goals for a long time. The problem is that success is not determined by hard work alone. It is also a function of passion and vision. Successful people see "it" before we see "it" and they are passionate about "it."

Read Genesis 37:5

_____

_____

_____

_____

_____

_____

_____

_____

Day 8

Morning Meditation:

*D*iligence makes the difference. Like water seeking its own level, our daily choices pave the way for our success at home and at work.

Read Hebrews 11:5; Deuteronomy 28:1-3

_____

_____

_____

_____

_____

_____

_____

_____

_____

_____

Day 9

Morning Mediation:

*F*reedom is short-lived. We are either snared by our own vices or we willfully surrender our freedom to a greater cause.

Read 2 Peter 2:19

_____

_____

_____

_____

_____

_____

_____

_____

_____

_____

Day 10

Morning Meditation:

What do you do when your spiritual gifting is in conflict with your position? May I suggest that either you redefine the position or seek a new one. To suppress or hide your gifts is of no benefit to you or the people you serve.

Read Matthew 5:15

_____

_____

_____

_____

_____

_____

_____

_____

Day 11

Morning Meditation:

*I*n the circle of life, there is only one path, but you may have to travel counter-clockwise to achieve your destination. Remember, the road to hell is paved with good intentions and false promises, but the path to good success requires us to travel some unpaved roads through some dark nights.

Read Matthew 7:14

_____

_____

_____

_____

_____

_____

_____

Day 12

Morning Meditation:

*F*ew people will ever realize their full human potential without God's divine intervention. In spite of our best plans and political connections, we need God to allow some things to happen to create opportunities for us and then grant us the courage to pursue what God has prepared for us.

Read Proverbs 3:5-6

_____

_____

_____

_____

_____

_____

_____

_____

Day 13

Morning Meditation:

There are many who subscribe to the belief that we have to adapt to our environment to survive – when in Rome, do as the Romans do. However, God sends us to dark places not to adapt, but to be the salt and light – to have dominion over the powers of darkness. So, have no fear of those who oppose you today and in the days to come. No weapon formed against you shall prosper!

Read Isaiah 54:17

Day 14

Morning Meditation:

*C*heck your motives. Some are driven to be better than others, while others are called to complete the task set before them. Driven people often lose sight of what's really important and fail to complete the tasks that matter. If anyone lacks wisdom, let him or her ask God for it. Selah.

Read James 1:5

_____

_____

_____

_____

_____

_____

_____

_____

Day 15

Morning Meditation:

$\mathcal{P}$reoccupation with how other people are being blessed by God can cause us to miss what God wants to do with our life. God knows us better than we know ourselves and He knows how big our cross should be. The bigger the blessing, the bigger the cross.

Read Malachi 3:14-17

_____

_____

_____

_____

_____

_____

_____

_____

_____

Day 16

Morning Meditation:

When your story is more about triumph than trial, don't be surprised when your crowd changes. God has to bring you out before you can be elevated. Remember to say 'excuse me' and 'thank you' as you move to the front row because God may need you to serve the same people in a new capacity.

Read Genesis 41:55

_____

_____

_____

_____

_____

_____

_____

_____

Day 17

Morning Meditation:

*W*hile it is important to plan for the future and set realistic goals and objectives, we must always be prepared to yield to divinely inspired paradigm shifts. In due season, God will move in a supernatural way and utterly reset the landscape of our lives. Don't grow weary in well doing even when it seems like no one cares. God is listening and watching.

Read 1 Corinthians 2:9

Day 18

Morning Meditation:

*W*e have all made choices that we regret, but successful people are able to turn these situations around for everyone involved. They begin by confessing their mistakes rather than trying to conceal them. God will take care of the rest!

Read James 5:16

_____

_____

_____

_____

_____

_____

_____

_____

Day 19

Morning Meditation:

*G*iving is one of the key principles in obtaining true wealth and yet it is a great stumbling block for so many. Some fear that they can't replace what they give and others only give in expectation of receiving more. God is not deceived and He blesses those who give sacrificially with a sincere heart.

Read Mark 10:21

_____

_____

_____

_____

_____

_____

_____

_____

Day 20

Morning Meditation:

" *K*issing up" really doesn't advance your agenda. Rather than being respected for who you are, you will be unappreciated and over-extended. Be your authentic self and be kind to everyone, especially people without political positions of influence. Whatever you do for the least (without drama), you have done so for Christ and will be rewarded!

Read Daniel 3:16-18, Mathew 25:40

_____

_____

_____

_____

_____

_____

_____

_____

Day 21

Morning Meditation:

*G*od really will supply all of your needs, but stop being double-minded. Surrender everything to God and learn to be content with what you already have. Count your blessings and give God praise for what He has already done!

Read Philippians 4:11-13

_____

_____

_____

_____

_____

_____

_____

_____

Day 22

Morning Meditation:

*W*hen you challenge the status quo and dare to help people redefine what normal looks like, you will be misunderstood. Press on anyway, the world needs more people like you.

Read Exodus 5:20-21

_____

_____

_____

_____

_____

_____

_____

_____

_____

_____

Day 23

Morning Meditation:

*G*reat days are planned the night before. You never know what you will face, but a good night's rest and a lot of prayer will help you awake without anxiety or fatigue.

Jeremiah 31:25-26

_____

_____

_____

_____

_____

_____

_____

_____

_____

Day 24

Morning Meditation:

*Y*our road to destiny is fraught with distractions and people with good intentions, but do not lose sight of your goal. Everyone who wants to be a part of your life or that benefits from what you do is not interested in celebrating with you. Conserve your energy and learn to say no because the closer you get to your destiny, the more you will have to fight!

Read Hebrews 12:1

_____

_____

_____

_____

_____

_____

_____

Day 25

Morning Meditation:

*D*on't be discouraged because the people you have helped have been promoted, while you appear to be ignored. God knows your good works and is going to elevate you higher than you ever imagined. Remember Joseph?

Read Genesis 40:14,23

Day 26

Morning Meditation:

*T*he ability to disassociate or disconnect is critical to spiritual maturity. When God speaks the words "leave" or "go" in Scripture, it is always followed with a greater promise and a stronger spiritual connection. Our problem is that it is so hard to say goodbye to yesterday. Listen, God is calling you to higher place.

Read Jonah 1:1-2

_____

_____

_____

_____

_____

_____

_____

_____

Making New Connections
Day 27

Morning Meditation:

*T*rust is the essential precondition upon which all real success depends. Yet, the Bible says, Put no trust in a neighbor; have no confidence in a friend; and guard the doors of your mouth from her who lies in your arms.

In whom then shall we trust for real success?

Read Micah 7:5.

_____

_____

_____

_____

_____

_____

_____

_____

_____

_____

Day 28

Morning Meditation:

*O*ur association with successful people is not what makes us successful, but rather our willingness to be held accountable to their authority.

Read Romans 13:2

_____

_____

_____

_____

_____

_____

_____

_____

_____

_____

_____

Day 29

Morning Meditation:

*G*od's gift to humanity is fellowship. We must be careful not to allow our positions or perceived power and influence over others prevent us from thinking more highly of others than ourselves. Real power and influence comes from remaining humble.

Read Luke 22:25-27

_____
_____
_____
_____
_____
_____
_____
_____
_____

Day 30

Morning Meditation:

*O*ur good success is rooted in the relationships we cultivate. This is why Jesus reminds us to not only love God, but our neighbors and our enemies. The harvest is plentiful, but few people are willing to invest quality time in relationships with people that are unable to give them immediate benefits. Gleaners harvest what they didn't plant, but if you need a greater harvest, then do the work!

Read Matthew 9:37

_____

_____

_____

_____

_____

_____

_____

Day 31

Morning Meditation:

$\mathcal{G}$od gave you the ability to create wealth so that you could be a blessing to others, not separate yourself from those with less or to think more highly of yourself. In fact, the poor are already blessed and have much to share with those who have much, but no joy.

Read Deuteronomy 8:17-18

_____

_____

_____

_____

_____

_____

_____

_____

Day 32

Morning Meditation:

*I*t is flattering to be seated in the VIP section and to be greeted by important people, but the real seat of honor is with the poor and the marginalized. Great men and women can dine with kings and queens, as well as with the homeless and those who are invisible to the rest of the world.

Read Luke 14:13-14

_____

_____

_____

_____

_____

_____

_____

_____

_____

Day 33

Morning Meditation:

$\mathscr{F}$orging mutually beneficial relationships outside your circle of influence and the willingness to accept advice from "outsiders" are the key elements to sustainable success. Focusing only on self-improvement or internal/organic growth will eventually lead to your demise.

Read Proverbs 13:20

_____

_____

_____

_____

_____

_____

_____

_____

_____

Day 34

Morning Meditation:

*K*nowing what invitations to accept and refuse are essential to our being in the right place at the right time. Most invitations are more about gratifying the one who extends the invitation, but a proper invitation should be to gratify those who accept the invitation.

Read Matthew 22:8-10

_____

_____

_____

_____

_____

_____

_____

_____

_____

Day 35

Morning Meditation:

*M*any of us are called for an interview, but few are chosen. God sends people in our lives daily to see if we are ready for what He has in store for us. How we live in our current position will determine our next position. Don't wait for the promotion or to be chosen for the next assignment; act like you already have it. If you can be faithful over a few things, then God will give you dominion over much more.

Read Mathew 25:23

_____

_____

_____

_____

_____

_____

_____

Day 36

Morning Meditation:

*P*ermanent positions and permanent enemies leave permanent scars. We must work daily to find common ground because our days on this earth are numbered. Consider the eternal consequences of your positions. How will you be remembered when this life is over and, if you must give an account of this life when it is all over, what will you say then?

Read Matthew 5:23-24

_____

_____

_____

_____

_____

_____

_____

_____

Day 37

Morning Meditation:

The less we try to control the people in our lives, the more control we have over our own lives. Everyone has to make his or her own mistakes. Better to prepare for the consequences rather than trying to prevent them from making the mistake.

Read Romans 15:1-2

_____

_____

_____

_____

_____

_____

_____

_____

Day 38

Morning Meditation:

*I*t is usually out of ignorance or narcissism that we attempt to reinvent the wheel, but when wisdom prevails, we seek counsel from those who are already doing what we hope to do.

Read Proverbs 15:22

_____

_____

_____

_____

_____

_____

_____

_____

_____

_____

Day 39

Morning Meditation:

*M*ake your request known and ask God to send someone who will journey with you to achieve your goal. Do not be surprised if God allows the devil to send you someone. Even those who oppose us help us to our goal by becoming our footstool. Caution: The battle is not ours!

Read Luke 20:42-43

_____

_____

_____

_____

_____

_____

_____

_____

_____

Day 40

Morning Meditation:

*B*roken hearts and failed relationships are the stops along the way to true success if we don't become bitter and stuck in the past. God knows the plans He has for us to prosper and not fail. It is time to fall in love with Jesus!

Read Matthew 11:28-30

_____

_____

_____

_____

_____

_____

_____

_____

_____

_____

Day 41

Morning Meditation:

*G*od begins the restoration process from the margins of life by redeeming people who are willing and able to challenge the way things have been done in the past. If you have been redeemed, then expect opposition from the people you are trying to help, as well as those who have blocked any restoration in the past.

Read Nehemiah 4:1-2

_____

_____

_____

_____

_____

_____

_____

_____

Day 42

Morning Meditation:

The work you do for others will speak for you when you are not in the room and will grant you access to places you never thought you would be. Just keep serving and trust that God will reward you in due season!

Read Proverbs 25:21-22

_____

_____

_____

_____

_____

_____

_____

_____

_____

Day 43

Morning Meditation:

When you think more highly of others, you open yourself to a lifetime of learning. People withhold valuable information from you when they don't believe you value them.

Read Romans 12:3

_____

_____

_____

_____

_____

_____

_____

_____

_____

_____

Day 44

Morning Meditation:

*G*reat teams make great team members, but great team members of weak teams languish and never reach their full potential. Your good success depends on whose team you are on. Join God's team because He promises greatness to your name and will not trade you when this life is over!

Read Proverbs 15:22

_____

_____

_____

_____

_____

_____

_____

_____

Day 45

Morning Meditation:

*J*ehovah pulls some relationships apart because He needs to reposition us for a fresh anointing. Don't try to hold on to people who want to leave, because Jehovah has a plan for them to prosper as well. Divine division is a good thing!

Read Genesis 13:8-10

_____

_____

_____

_____

_____

_____

_____

_____

_____

_____

Day 46

Morning Meditation:

*P*rotect and pursue your purpose by a establishing a firm foundation of small-group Bible study and regular prayer meetings. Individual belief and self-reliance is not enough!

Read Hebrews 10:25

_____

_____

_____

_____

_____

_____

_____

_____

_____

_____

Counting the Cost
Day 47

Morning Meditation:

Thank God for taking some things away from you. To be fruitful, a fruit tree must be pruned so that its root system can grow stronger and support the fruitful growth of the top portion. Remember the fig tree that Jesus cursed. Leaves without fruit brings condemnation.

Read Mark 11:12-14

_____

_____

_____

_____

_____

_____

_____

_____

_____

Day 48

Morning Meditation:

*U*nmet expectations and false hopes are the seeds of despair and our anxiety. Build your hope on things eternal and believe that the best is yet to come!

Read Philippians 4:4-9

_____

_____

_____

_____

_____

_____

_____

_____

_____

_____

_____

Day 49

Morning Meditation:

$\mathcal{O}$ur personal moral failure causes us to see the failure in others and in the organizations of which we are a part. We must first be true to ourselves before we can see things from a positive perspective.

Read John 8:7-10

_____

_____

_____

_____

_____

_____

_____

_____

_____

_____

Day 50

Morning Meditation.

*M*ost of what people hear us say was actually never spoken by us. People actually understand and remember about 3 out of 100 words we say. The rest is all non-verbal; what we look like, how we say it, when we say it, why we said it, our position, etc.

Read 1 Corinthians 13:1

_____

_____

_____

_____

_____

_____

_____

_____

_____

Day 51

Morning Meditation:

*S*uccessful people ask the right questions. Although there are no dumb questions, Jesus was careful to respond to some questions with rebuke and others with a blessing. Whenever you ask a question of someone, you open the window of your soul. Be careful how you ask questions if you want to be successful in this life.

Read Mathew 4:6-7

_____

_____

_____

_____

_____

_____

_____

_____

Day 52

Morning Meditation:

In your pursuit of wealth (not income) you will discover it cannot be obtained by working long hours or seeking the highest paying job, but rather in the pursuit of excellence. Those who excel in what they do tend to work fewer hours and are usually self-employed, with multiple income streams.

Read Joshua 24:14

_____

_____

_____

_____

_____

_____

_____

_____

Day 53

Morning Meditation:

*W*hen you have been anointed to give, there will be many who despise you and the work of your hands. But, give anyway; God wants to keep on blessing you and the enemy wants to stop you from giving so that he can block your blessing. This is why we are to give in secret so that we will not fall into the temptation of pride.

Read Matthew 6:4

_____

_____

_____

_____

_____

_____

_____

_____

Day 54

Morning Meditation:

*S*ome try to buy leadership positions with their wealth and some try to assume these positions because of the family into which they were born, but God chooses leaders from among the least likely to succeed, according to their heart.

Read Romans 12:3

Day 55

Morning Meditation:

A good man leaves an inheritance for his own grandchildren, but a great man is a blessing to many families and will not be easily forgotten in the generations to come. Whatever we have done for the least, we have done also unto God. Let us make our life one worth remembering!

Read Genesis 22:17-18

_____

_____

_____

_____

_____

_____

_____

_____

_____

Day 56

Morning Meditation:

*T*is a common belief that we must reward ourselves before we can give to others, but personal rewards are far greater if you invest in others first – even when you don't have enough time and resources for yourself. Seek ye first the Kingdom of God rather than trying to build your own kingdom!

Read Matthew 6:31-34

_____

_____

_____

_____

_____

_____

_____

_____

Day 57

Morning Meditation:

$\int$ acrifice and success are two sides of a coin. One cannot be had without the other. Many will sacrifice others to achieve their success. Few will make personal sacrifices for their own success. One sacrificed Himself for the success of all. Thank you, Jesus!

Read Mark 8:36

_____

_____

_____

_____

_____

_____

_____

_____

_____

Day 58

Morning Meditation:

*W*hen the repayment of debt consumes our energy and limits our creativity, we have surrendered our divine purpose for being. Find your purpose and restructure your debt.

Read Leviticus 25:35-37, Deuteronomy 15:1-2

_____

_____

_____

_____

_____

_____

_____

_____

_____

Day 59

Morning Meditation:

We can only be robbed of our blessings by feeding our vanity. Learning to decline certain invitations and refusing secret pleasures is the beginning of good success. Be sure that God is getting the glory out of your life.

Read Ecclesiastes 2:10-11

_____

_____

_____

_____

_____

_____

_____

_____

_____

_____

Day 60

Morning Meditation:

*W*e must be careful not to let our possessions or lack of possessions rob us of our joy. We are worth more than our net worth!

Read Luke 12:19-21

_____

_____

_____

_____

_____

_____

_____

_____

_____

_____

Day 61

Morning Meditation:

*Y*our brand determines how much you are worth to others. What you wear, how you treat others and the words you speak determine your brand. You may want to reevaluate your brand if people are consistently undervaluing you.

Read John 13:35

_____

_____

_____

_____

_____

_____

_____

_____

_____

Day 62

Morning Meditation:

*P*ublic life does not have private choices. Choose wisely before you accept leadership positions. That which is acceptable and normal in private life becomes the subject of criticism and sometimes, heated debate. This is why the Bible cautions us to remain humble and slow to speak, but the day will come when God will exalt you and give you the words to speak.

Read Luke 21:15

_____

_____

_____

_____

_____

_____

Pressing to the Mark
Day 63

Morning Meditation:

*V*isionary Leadership emerges at times of distress and great tribulation, and they are most likely to be of humble birth. This type of leader is always a threat to those who presume leadership to be a birthright. The "legacy leader" tells us about their past success, whereas the "visionary leader" tells us about our future hope.

Read Nehemiah 2:19

_____

_____

_____

_____

_____

_____

_____

_____

Day 64

Morning Meditation:

The anointed appear ordinary until there is extraordinary conflict. Whether by storm, flood or fire, the anointed are covered by the blood and shall come through the conflict with joy and greater authority!

Read Romans 8:38-39

_____

_____

_____

_____

_____

_____

_____

_____

_____

Day 65

Morning Meditation:

God's plan for humanity is like a long-distance relay race with an uncertain ending. If we drop the baton handed to us from the prior generation, then we must pick it up anyway and finish our part of the race and pray that the next generation will make up for the lost time. Whatever you do, please don't stop running – our future depends on it!

Read Hebrews 12:1

_____

_____

_____

_____

_____

_____

_____

_____

Day 66

Morning Meditation:

*M*any are called, but few are chosen. When you are God's choice, you will receive promotions you didn't expect and enemies you never knew before the promotion. Fear not, the Lord is with you and you will prevail if you remember how you were elevated – not by your strength, but by God's will alone.

Read Zechariah 4:6

_____

_____

_____

_____

_____

_____

_____

_____

Day 67

Morning Meditation:

There are some things we carry that make our victory lap feel like we lost the race, but do not be deceived. You are a winner even though you went through hell to get where you are now. Tell your story!

Read Romans 8:35-37

_____

_____

_____

_____

_____

_____

_____

_____

_____

_____

Day 68

Morning Meditation:

*I*t takes more energy and determination to come from behind, especially when those who publicly support you whisper behind your back that you can't do it. Ignore the talk, fight the temptations, and celebrate the small triumphs. Victory is yours, and vengeance is the Lord's. When it is all over, you will not have to fight this battle again.

Read Song of Solomon 2:15

_____

_____

_____

_____

_____

_____

_____

Day 69

Morning Meditation:

*F*ear from our past haunts our future, but God has not given us a spirit of fear. Behold, old things have passed away and God wants to do a new thing in your life.

Read 2 Timothy 1:7; 1 John 1:6-7

_____

_____

_____

_____

_____

_____

_____

_____

_____

_____

_____

Day 70

Morning Meditation:

*D*on't let another person's anger and frustration cause you to lose sight of your goals and your personal perspective. Keep an open mind!

Read Ephesians 4:25-27

_____

_____

_____

_____

_____

_____

_____

_____

_____

_____

Day 71

Morning Meditation:

The plans of men cannot destroy, derail or distract you from what God has planned for you. God already knew what mistakes you would make and how those who you put confidence in would betray you. As long as you trust in the Lord and diligently seek Him, the best is still yet to come. Walk with God!

Read Hebrews 11:6

_____

_____

_____

_____

_____

_____

_____

Day 72

Morning Meditation:

*F*ear not! Have compassion on those who oppose you because they are only striking poses, but the Lord will not bless the work of their hands. Remain faithful and in a posture of prayer and you will prevail!

Read Psalm 28:204

_____

_____

_____

_____

_____

_____

_____

_____

_____

_____

Day 73

Morning Meditation:

Seldom is it clear as to where God is leading us or how long it will take to get there, but many are the blessings along the journey if we can overcome those who oppose us. Opposition will rise from those who have kept us in bondage and those who fear that we are about to occupy their positions, but the battle is not ours. Keep it moving!

Read Matthew 10:14

_____

_____

_____

_____

_____

_____

_____

_____

Day 74

Morning Meditation:

R eal leaders lead with limited visibility, a firm resolve and great expectations. We can only fully recognize great leadership when they take us to the promised destination. Fools over-promise and give up on the journey because they are unable to convince people of something they don't believe themselves. Hope is not the same as hype!

Read Exodus 14:10-13

Day 75

Morning Meditation:

*N*ecessity is the creator of our realized existence and yet before we were born, God knew the plans He had for us to prosper and not fail. This is how we know that all things work together for good to them who love God, to them who are the called according to his purpose.

Read Romans 8:28

Day 76

Morning Meditation:

*G*reat moments in life are usually the result of a series of incidents over which we have very little control. Some call this luck or good timing, while others actually convince themselves that it was their own political connections. I call it the hand of God. When we step out on faith to do something that is not self-serving, God creates *kairos* moments for us.

Read Genesis 12:1-3

_____

_____

_____

_____

_____

_____

_____

Day 77

Morning Meditation:

*C*onsistency, character and commitment will sustain you, but may not elevate you like charisma and connections do. Nevertheless, be faithful until the end because the reward is promised to those who endure until the end.

Read Romans 5:1-5

_____

_____

_____

_____

_____

_____

_____

_____

_____

Day 78

Morning Meditation:

*B*lind ambition and a need to prove you can succeed against all odds – all by yourself – is a trick of the devil. Better to be humble and do what you can with what you have until God opens the door for something greater. Surely there is a crown for those who can endure in hardships and for those who are not so easily offended.

Read Mathew 4:8-10

_____

_____

_____

_____

_____

_____

_____

Day 79

Morning Meditation:

Living the blessed life and receiving all that God has in store for us requires us to deny the persistent impulse to acquire things that we can obtain by our own effort or credit.

Read Psalm 23:1

_____
_____
_____
_____
_____
_____
_____
_____
_____
_____

Day 80

Morning Meditation:

*W*hen the enemy is not able to block you from your destiny, be careful. The next move of the enemy is to try to push your past your destiny by changing your confidence into arrogance. Remember, it is not by your might, but by God's power and His timing. Be still and wait for God before you make your next move.

Read Zechariah 4:6

_____

_____

_____

_____

_____

_____

_____

_____

Day 81

Morning Meditation:

D oubt can deprive us of our blessings. No matter how bad our situation has gotten, we can be assured that the best is yet to come if our steps are ordered by God and not fear.

Read Matthew 14:28-31

_____

_____

_____

_____

_____

_____

_____

_____

_____

_____

Day 82

Morning Meditation:

$\mathcal{B}$e clear about your divine assignments and appointments and do not let the ordinary tasks of life interfere with the extraordinary blessings God wants to bestow upon you. Start today with the end in mind!

Read Matthew 8:21-22

_____

_____

_____

_____

_____

_____

_____

_____

_____

Day 83

Morning Meditation:

*W*hen you pray for blessings and to be used by God, why are you so surprised when you encounter envy, jealousy, and gossip? Your success draws attention to the failure and insecurity of others, but soon you will even be a blessing to your haters. Keep pressing to the mark of the high calling!

Read Genesis 37:5-11

_____

_____

_____

_____

_____

_____

_____

_____

Day 84

Morning Meditation:

Some say that success and familiarity breed contempt. Yet, our success is dependent on forming relationships with people we don't always like or with which we agree. Contempt is always there whether you succeed or not, so don't be discouraged from pursuing your goals!

Read 1 Peter 3:8-9

_____

_____

_____

_____

_____

_____

_____

_____

Day 85

Morning Meditation:

Looks can be deceiving. When we decide to live and not die, others cannot see how much we have suffered and the obstacles we have overcome. Encourage others by telling your story and how you made it!

Read Psalms 107:1-3

_____

_____

_____

_____

_____

_____

_____

_____

_____

Day 86

Morning Meditation:

*O*ur anxiety about where we are going and how we will get there makes it impossible to walk with God. Focus on living each day in a way that glorifies God and tomorrow will take of itself. The promotions will come and your enemies will become steppingstones. Keep rising to the top.

Psalm 110:1

_____

_____

_____

_____

_____

_____

_____

_____

Day 87

Morning Meditation:

Take your mask off, and then others will, too. The fear of letting people know who you really are only delays the inevitable. Be accepted or rejected for who you are!

Read Psalm 139:14

_____

_____

_____

_____

_____

_____

_____

_____

_____

Day 88

Morning Meditation:

*S*uccess is not rooted in mountain-top experiences, but in the valley of human despair. It is in the most difficult times of life that our masks come off and the seeds of success are planted. Wait for your harvest before you climb the next mountain!

Read Matthew 17:1-9

_____

_____

_____

_____

_____

_____

_____

_____

Day 89

Morning Meditation:

*R*esistance to change is not always a bad thing. God uses resistance to move us a to new place physically and/or spiritually. Failure to respond to resistance is always a bad thing. Be strong and deal with the obstacles in your way!

Read Exodus 14:10-14

_____
_____
_____
_____
_____
_____
_____
_____
_____

Day 90

Morning Meditation:

*T*here are some people in your life who just can't celebrate your success because of their own personal failures and present fears. Pray for them and celebrate with them when you can.

Read John 9:34

_____

_____

_____

_____

_____

_____

_____

_____

_____

Day 91

Morning Meditation:

*Y*our biggest supporters are behind the scenes and seldom reveal themselves, but be cautious of those who seek you out. Choose wisely those in whom you confide.

Read Proverbs 13:20

_____

_____

_____

_____

_____

_____

_____

_____

_____

_____

Day 92

Morning Meditation:

*F*ear and doubt are the primary spirits that weaken us and prevent us from receiving our blessings. These spirits can literally make us feel disconnected from God's love, but God will come looking for us and give us a spirit of knowledge to discern His voice. Wait for it!

Read Genesis 3:8-10

_____

_____

_____

_____

_____

_____

_____

_____

_____

_____

Day 93

Morning Meditation:

*M*ountain-top experiences breed intense jealousy, hatred and discrimination. Dream anyway. If God shows it to you, then it will come to pass and your enemies will be nothing more than steppingstones and distant memories.

Read Numbers 12:2

_____

_____

_____

_____

_____

_____

_____

_____

_____

_____

The Winner's Circle
Day 94

Morning Meditation:

*O*n our way to the winner's circle, it is hard to find people who will pray with us, but many will prey on us. In fact, some of our best friends (even family) will try to keep us from going to church or from gathering with people who know who we are in Christ. Press your way to the winner's circle today!

Read Hebrews 10:25

_____

_____

_____

_____

_____

_____

_____

Day 95

Morning Meditation:

*S*ometimes we can get stuck complaining about our past and how things should have happened. With such a mindset, we will miss the fact that the world around us has changed and our enemies have moved on. The winner's circle is finally in our grasp, but some of us will die outside that circle because we simply refuse to let go of the bondage of their past.

Read James 4:8

_____
_____
_____
_____
_____
_____
_____
_____

Day 96

Morning Meditation:

*I*n the Winner's Circle we find time to re-discover meaning and purpose in friendships that have developed throughout our journey. We stop seeing people as a means to an end, but rather they become the end goal. Love thy neighbor as thy self and love your enemies even more.

Read Mathew 5:44

_____

_____

_____

_____

_____

_____

_____

_____

_____

Day 97

Morning Meditation:

Living life in the winner's circle means coming to a place where our beginning meets our end, i. e. we discover our purpose for living. Unfortunately, most of our life is consumed with choosing between the lesser of two evils or engaging in activities as a means to an uncertain end. The challenge is to stop looking at life as a straight line that continues indefinitely, but rather as a continuous loop that cannot be disconnected from our beginning.

Read Jeremiah 29:11.

_____

_____

_____

_____

_____

_____

Day 98

Morning Meditation:

Living life in the winner's circle can be lonely at times and it may even be stressful if you forget how and why you have made it there. Many will question your path and may even demand to see your birth certificate or demand a recount. Still others will hurl insults and make threats, but remember what Jesus said, "Father forgive them, they don't know what they are doing."

Read Luke 23:34

_____

_____

_____

_____

_____

_____

_____

Day 99

Morning Meditation:

Living life in the winner's circle requires us to examine our failed relationship with money and the source of our wealth. God will not only give us our daily bread, God also wants to bless us beyond anything we could ever think or imagine. The challenge is staying in the winner's circle. It is our place of promise!

Read Matthew 19:21-22

_____

_____

_____

_____

_____

_____

_____

_____

Day 100

Morning Meditation:

Living life in the winner's circle requires us to overcome the shame of our failures and the boldness to return to the place where we are loved. We must not be discouraged by those who claim to have never failed or those who secretly wish they could have lived the lives we once did. A crown of glory is waiting for us. Claim your victory!

Read 1 Peter 5:4.

_____

_____

_____

_____

_____

_____

_____

Author Bio

*R*ev. Sidney Williams is the pastor of Bethel AME Church in Morristown, N.J., and is a graduate of Howard University, The Wharton Business School and Wesley Theological Seminary. Pastor Williams caries a prophetic mantle that distinguishes him as a remarkable visionary who has made a powerful impact in the faith and business communities. He preaches, lectures, teaches, encourages and strengthens the faith of people across the globe from Los Angeles to New York and from the Caribbean to Africa. His work focuses on empowering both believers and non-believers to work together to make the world a better place for generations to come.

He is the husband of Teresa, and a devoted father to his precious little ladies, Nicole, Sarah, Hannah, and his son, Sidney III.

Need additional copies?

To order more copies of

contact CertaPublishing.com

☐ Order online at:
CertaPublishing.com/MorningMeditations

☐ Call 855-77-CERTA or

☐ Email Info@CertaPublishing.com